Kathleen Lee Dong

COLLECTIVE NARCISSISM

How the culture of "me" has changed us

Introduction

While individual narcissism has long been the subject of psychological investigation, rarely is consideration given to how the whole of society leads us to hold attitudes that expose us to the narcissist trap. In the current socio-cultural context, marked by a profound interplay between individual and collective identities, the concept of collective narcissism is beginning to become more than a reflection, but a topic of fundamental relevance for understanding contemporary social and cultural dynamics.

Collective narcissism offers a perspective to examine how the norms, values and behaviors of an entire community can be influenced by narcissistic hegemony.

Collective narcissism, as a social phenomenon, transcends the individual, manifesting itself as an issue of collective relevance precisely because it permeates our entire cultural consciousness, thus delineating a landscape in which the relentless pursuit of approval and visibility becomes a shared practice.

In an age when social legitimacy is achieved through the display and celebration of ego, the culture of "me" takes shape as a collective rhetoric that shapes our daily interactions and redefines the meaning of community.

Questioning collective narcissism is important not only to recognize its deleterious effects, but also to understand its sociocultural and psychological roots. This phenomenon can be interpreted as a response to the alienation and isolation that characterize modernity. In a world where interpersonal relationships are mediated by screens and digital platforms, narcissism becomes a defense mechanism, a social survival strategy that seeks to rebuild a sense of belonging in a world that seems fragmented and lacking in authenticity.

From a sociological perspective, collective narcissism invites reflection on the ways in which social structures influence individual identities. The increasing emphasis on individualism, typical of contemporary societies, has given rise to a context in which authentic relationships are replaced by superficial interactions and competition. Social media, in this scenario, act as amplifiers of narcissistic dynamics, creating an environment in which personal value is measured in terms of likes and endorsements. This generates a vicious cycle in which self-aggrandizement becomes the norm and genuine relationships are sacrificed on the altar of self-exposure.

From an anthropological perspective, collective narcissism raises questions about the ways in which contemporary cultures shape identities. Cultural practices and collective narratives are increasingly influenced by the logic of narcissism, and authenticity is often sacrificed in favor of an idealized representation of the self. In this context, the norms and values that once fostered community and interpersonal bonding fade away, giving way to continuous self-assertion that results in relentless competition.

On a psychological level, collective narcissism can result in a disconnect between the self and others. When the power of the collective ego overrides individuality, it creates an environment in which empathy is replaced by rivalry. The "me" culture, fueled by the use of social media, generates a constant comparison between the lives of individuals, fueling a distortion of reality in which external validation becomes the sole measure of personal worth. This phenomenon has increasingly led us to superficial interpersonal relationships, growing dissatisfaction and an increase in mental health problems, such as anxiety and depression.

It will also be crucial to examine how collective narcissism interacts with power structures and political dynamics. Charismatic and narcissistic leaders can exploit the culture of collective narcissism to consolidate their power by manipulating the emotions and perceptions of the masses. The polarization and tribalism that characterize modern societies can certainly be interpreted through the lens of collective narcissism: the need to belong to a group that asserts its superiority, often at the expense of others, becomes a socially accepted and incentivized behavior.

This small treatise aims to examine collective narcissism to encourage the exploration of how it manifests in contemporary culture, but also to investigate its repercussions on individuals' psychological well-being and social cohesion.

The hope is to stimulate reflection on this issue, inviting us all to question how collective narcissism shapes not only the way we live, but also the way we think and feel.

In a world where personal worth seems to be measured by social (and social) approval, it is imperative to ask: at what cost? What are the consequences of a culture that celebrates the individual and ignores the foundations of authentic human connection?

Chapter 1: What is Collective Narcissism?

In the context of contemporary culture, which is characterized by a continuous quest for visibility and approval, the concept of collective narcissism has acquired a new dimension in recent decades. This phenomenon is not limited to a small, defined group, but permeates the entire society, shaping our daily interactions and our perception of individual worth. We have become unwilling participants in this narcissistic ballet in which the "me" prevails over the "we," generating a generalized disregard for others.

Definition of Collective Narcissism

Collective narcissism can be defined as a cultural tendency in which individuals' aspirations, emotions and identities are dominated by self-aggrandizement and a constant search for recognition. While individual narcissism may manifest in self-exaltation behaviors, collective narcissism results in a shared narrative in which the group identifies itself through mutual admiration and comparison with others. This phenomenon manifests itself in behaviors ranging from superficiality in personal relationships to unbridled competition for social approval, all fueled by the echo of social media and image culture.

Above all, collective narcissism is not a characteristic of more isolated or marginal groups, it is not ascribable only to certain age groups or professions or incomes or genders, far from it: it is an attribute that runs through all segments of society. This implies that every individual, to some extent, is involved in this dynamic, contributing to a culture in which self-centeredness has become the norm. The direct consequence of this tendency is the creation of a social environment in which disinterest in others becomes almost inevitable.

History and Development of the Concept

The concept of collective narcissism has emerged in the context of profound social and cultural changes. Although the origins of narcissism can be traced to the psychoanalytic theories of Sigmund Freud, its development in the collective context has been influenced by the emergence of mass culture and digitization. Since the 1980s, with the increasing spread of mass media and then social media, collective narcissism has taken hold, reaching a new intensity in contemporary culture.

Social platforms, such as Facebook and Instagram, not only facilitate the sharing of content, but also nurture a culture of comparison, in which individuals continually measure themselves against the successes and life images of others. This dynamic has led to a pervasive valorization of appearance, replacing authentic relationships with superficial interactions in which authenticity is sacrificed in favor of a curated and idealized image.

Collective narcissism has historical roots that extend across different cultures and periods. A pertinent example is the personality cults that characterized totalitarian regimes in the 20th century. These phenomena created collective narratives that justified leader worship and the alienation of dissenting voices, establishing a culture of conformity and disregard for individual freedoms.

In more recent contexts, the phenomenon has manifested itself through mass movements and youth cultures, where collective identity has been built around ideals of success and social status. Music festivals, political rallies and activist groups, while born of noble intentions, can easily fall victim to collective narcissism, turning into displays of ego and challenges for social recognition rather than genuine opportunities for dialogue and change.

A further example can be found in fashion and entertainment culture, where the representation of the "ideal" is constantly propagated, fueling frustration and inadequacy among individuals. Celebrities, through their access to platforms of global visibility, set unattainable standards that everyone tries to imitate, creating a vicious cycle of competition and disregard for the well-being of others.

Nor can we forget that the educational model followed by many parents in recent generations has often been characterized by an excessive focus on their children's self-esteem, which may have fostered the creation of a context in which the individual self becomes the central axis of identity. Parents, in some cases, were encouraged to raise their children in a climate of constant gratification, in which every small accomplishment was celebrated as a great success, leaving no room for frustration or failure. This kind of approach may have contributed to the development of a sense of grandiosity or an expectation of constant approval, which is then manifested in social dynamics and interpersonal relationships, also reflected in the use of social media.

In this context, the issue of collective narcissism should be read not only as an individual phenomenon but as a reflection of broader cultural trends. Parents who raised their children during the economic and technological boom years, for example, may have transmitted, consciously or unconsciously, values related to personal success and appearance rather than authenticity and emotional connection.

But a sociological and anthropological approach to the phenomenon of collective narcissism offers a more nuanced and less deterministic view than mere psychological heredity. The socio-economic context of the last few decades has seen a rapid acceleration of individualism, fueled by the neoliberal idea of meritocracy and the emphasis on personal abilities as the only key to success. This has promoted a competitive culture in which image and self-promotion become essential tools for asserting oneself in a society increasingly saturated by information and appearance.

The explosion of social media in recent decades has then further exacerbated these trends. Digital platforms have created a public arena in which identity is constantly being performed, and where visibility is directly linked to success. In an environment where being seen and approved by others becomes a social currency, collective narcissism takes root as an almost inevitable response to the pressures of a society that constantly demands attention and recognition.

Another element to consider is the economic structure within which these psychological and cultural dynamics operate. Late-modern capitalism is based on the idea of the consumer as the protagonist, encouraging a constant need for recognition and distinction. This results in the continuous exposure of the self through digital tools, with a constant emphasis on self-promotion and individualism. Social competition, both real and perceived, thus becomes a powerful stimulus for the strengthening of narcissism at the collective level.

This dynamic can be seen in various aspects of daily life: from careers to consumption, from interpersonal relationships to lifestyle choices. People are driven to present an idealized version of themselves, partly to conform to external standards of success, partly to satisfy their own psychological needs for approval and recognition. Collective narcissism thus emerges as a product of a cultural system that rewards ego, visibility and self-promotion.

And if family and cultural dynamics have created the conditions for the emergence of collective narcissism, the technological infrastructure has acted as an accelerator. Social media not only provide platforms for expression, but also incentivize specific narcissistic behaviors through reward systems that gratify and reinforce self-aggrandizing attitudes. Digital social interactions have thus turned into performances visible to a wide audience, incentivizing the creation of identities that adhere to aesthetic and behavioral parameters dictated by the logic of the algorithm.

In this sense, collective narcissism is thus a set of cultural and technological mechanisms that encourage self-centeredness and the continuous search for external confirmation. A system of social values and expectations that spans generations and adapts to technological and cultural changes.

Contemporary society, with its emphasis on individualism, personal success and self-promotion, has made collective narcissism an almost inevitable response to systemic pressures.

In sum, our culture, which is increasingly oriented toward self-aggrandizement, calls for a critical analysis and rethinking of the core values that shape our relationships. Recognizing this trend is not enough; it is also necessary to initiate a dialogue on how to address and defuse collective narcissism, promoting empathy and human connection as antidotes to a culture that often forgets the importance of the "other."

Chapter 2: The Signs of Collective Narcissism.

Collective narcissism is the sum of a number of behaviors and attitudes that have become increasingly prevalent in contemporary society.

I will try to clarify how these signs are not simply individual manifestations, but reflect a collective condition that has profound implications for our relationships and the social fabric as a whole.

Common Behaviors and Attitudes

Signs of collective narcissism are evident in many aspects of daily life. Superficiality is one of the most common behaviors associated with this tendency. In a world where appearance matters more than content, the evaluation of people and situations is often based on superficial criteria, such as physical appearance, social prestige, or the number of followers on social media. This superficiality results in interactions that prioritize image over meaning, leading to fragile and insubstantial relationships.

Another distinctive sign is constant attention-seeking. Individuals, driven by the need to be seen and approved, develop behaviors that may appear excessive or self-indulgent. This attention-seeking can manifest itself in various ways: from excessive use of social media to share details of daily life, to public performances aimed at gaining acclaim and recognition. This behavior is not only limited to individuals, but also permeates group dynamics: communities seek to stand out through self-aggrandizement and competition for attention.

Signs of collective narcissism are evident in the way we relate to others. Empathy, a fundamental value in human interactions, is often replaced by indifference to the needs and emotions of others. This disregard for others is not only a symptom of individual selfishness, but reflects a social condition in which people feel entitled to put their own needs and desires above all else, to the detriment of collective well-being.

The Culture of "Me" and Self-Celebration in Social Media

The term "'me' culture" has emerged to describe a social environment in which self-aggrandizement has become the norm. In this culture, the individual is constantly exposed to messages that promote the importance of personal success and image. Social media, in particular, has played a key role in perpetuating this dynamic by providing platforms where users can construct and present curated versions of themselves.

Through posts, photos, and videos, individuals seek approval and recognition. The value of content is often measured in terms of likes and shares, creating a positive feedback loop that encourages increasingly narcissistic behavior. In this context, the line between private and public life becomes blurred; what was once considered intimate is now exhibited as a form of social legitimacy.

Obsession with one's image leads to constant comparison with others, generating anxiety and dissatisfaction. The question is no longer "who am I?" but "how do I appear to others?" This shift in the perception of individual identity is at the root of a number of psychological problems, including depression and anxiety, which affect not only individuals but also interpersonal relationships.

The culture of competition and confrontation

We live in a time when comparison is inevitable: whether it is in careers, relationships or physical aspects, society encourages us to compete and measure our worth by the successes of others. This competitive environment, fueled by social media and public narratives, drives individuals to try to outdo others, rather than to collaborate and build meaningful relationships.

Competition is not only limited to professional or personal spheres; it also extends to consumer culture, an area in which brands compete for consumer attention. This phenomenon leads to a continuous search for novelty and originality: the value of experiences is measured by how unique and unexpected they are. In this context, individuals feel compelled to perform and exhibit lifestyles that live up to social expectations, which contributes to a perpetuating cycle of dissatisfaction and competition.

The culture of competition, then, results in a social environment in which the collective ego prevails over shared humanity. People become mere pawns in a game of prestige, in which personal success is the only goal. This leads not only to increased social pressure, but also to decreased authenticity in relationships, as individuals fear showing vulnerabilities or weaknesses, believing them to be indicators of failure.

Superficiality, attention-seeking, "me" culture, and constant competition are thus symptoms of a society that has cast aside fundamental values such as empathy, collaboration, and authenticity. Recognizing and addressing these signs is the first step toward a deeper understanding of how collective narcissism has changed us and how we can work to rebuild more meaningful relationships based on mutual respect and honesty.

Self-Assessment Test

Instructions: For each statement, respond by selecting the score that best represents your agreement, using the following scale:

- **1**: Mai
- **2**: Rarely
- **3**: Sometimes
- **4**: Often
- **5**: Always

Section 1: Search for Attention

1. I feel the need to frequently share my successes on social media.
2. I worry a lot about how I appear to others.
3. I actively try to attract the attention of others in social situations.
4. I feel dissatisfied if my social media posts don't get enough likes or comments.
5. I often talk about myself in conversations without paying attention to others.

Section 2: Superficiality in Relationships.

1. I find superficial relationships easier to handle than deep ones.
2. I often judge people by their physical appearance or popularity.
3. I care more about the number of friends or followers I have rather than the quality of relationships.
4. I often feel I am competing with others for social approval.
5. 10.I prefer to interact with people who share images and achievements similar to mine.

Section 3: Competition and Comparison

1. I frequently compare myself with others to evaluate my success.
2. 12.I feel I have to be "the best" in everything I do.
3. 13.If someone else is successful, I feel a sense of envy or competition.

4.   14. I tend to downplay the successes of others in order to feel better about myself.
5.   15. I participate in discussions that focus on success and social status.

Section 4: Indifference to Others

1.   16. Sometimes I feel that others are not as important as I am.
2.   17. I struggle to show empathy toward the difficulties of others.
3.   18. I care more about my image than about the needs of people close to me.
4.   19. I often don't care about the welfare of others unless it has an impact on me.
5.   20. When I listen to someone talk about their problems, my mind wanders to my own thoughts.

Interpretation of Results

Total Score: Sum the scores obtained for each statement.

- **20-40 points: Low level of collective narcissism**
  You seem to have a good awareness of your relationships and a balance between your needs and those of others. Your ability to empathize and interact authentically is evident.
- **41-60 points: Moderate level of collective narcissism**
  You are aware of the "me" culture around you and may sometimes find yourself seeking attention or comparing yourself to others. Consider reflecting on how your actions may affect your relationships.
- **61-80 points: High level of collective narcissism**
  You may be strongly influenced by seeking social approval and superficiality in relationships. It is important to examine how your behavior may

be moving you away from authentic and meaningful relationships.

- **81-100 points: Extremely high level of collective narcissism**
  Your life seems to be centered on attention-seeking and self-aggrandizement, at the expense of relationships and the well-being of others. It is critical to reflect on these tendencies and consider working to improve your empathy and interactions with others.

Conclusion

This test is a small tool for reflection and awareness. If you have discovered that you have narcissistic tendencies, this is not a sign of failure, but rather an opportunity to grow. Self-reflection is the first step in overcoming collective narcissism (and more).

Self-reflection test

This section is designed to help you more deeply assess your personal narcissism and relationships since having answered the previous test you are probably now wondering about other aspects of your character. Answer the following questions honestly, reflecting on your experiences and behaviors.

Reflection Questions

1. **To what extent do you think your happiness depends on the approval of others?**
   (Write a short reflection.)
2. **Do you often feel dissatisfied with your relationships? If yes, why?**
   (Write a short reflection.)
3. **When someone shares a success, how do you feel?**
   Happy for them
   b) Indifferent
   c) Envious
   d) Other (specify)

4. **Reflect on a time when you sought the attention of others. What prompted you to do so?**
   (Write a short reflection.)
5. **Have you ever noticed that your behaviors tend to focus more on yourself rather than on others? In what situations does this happen?**
   (Write a short reflection.)
6. **Have you ever felt uncomfortable or anxious if you do not get the attention you desire? If yes, recount an episode.**
   (Write a short reflection.)
7. **What are the things that make you proud of yourself? Do you think there is a balance between your pride and your ability to appreciate others?**
   (Write a short reflection.)
8. **Have you ever had difficulty showing vulnerability in your relationships? If yes, what are your fears?**
   (Write a short reflection.)

These reflection questions invite you to examine your behavior in a more personal context. Take the time to answer truthfully and thoroughly. Remember that self-awareness is critical.

After completing this section, take a moment to reread your answers. Think about how often your thoughts and behaviors reflect narcissism. If you notice troubling tendencies or a strong focus on you, consider talking to a professional who can help you explore these dynamics and develop strategies to improve your relationships.

Chapter 3: The role of social media

In a world increasingly connected and influenced by social media, the self-assessment tests presented in the previous chapters are not just an academic exercise, but an opportunity to reflect on how our habits and behaviors are shaped by contemporary culture. The self-analysis promoted by these tools allows us to recognize narcissistic tendencies and understand how they manifest themselves in our daily lives. It is crucial to question how collective narcissism is intertwined with the dynamics of social media, as this phenomenon has radically transformed our social interactions, creating an environment in which approval-seeking and self-aggrandizement are now central elements of our existence.

Social platforms, since their inception, have revolutionized how we communicate, transforming the way we construct and perceive our identities. The interactive nature of these tools facilitates not only contact between individuals, but also an incessant flow of information and feedback that help shape our self-perception.

Social platforms were designed to facilitate and optimize interaction among users. However, this interaction, while having positive potential, has also contributed to the emergence of our collective narcissism. A key aspect of this process is the ability of platforms to incentivize behaviors that lead to incessant approval-seeking. The visibility of posts, the ability to receive comments and "likes," and the creation of viral content all fuel personal gratification through social interaction.

The design of social platforms, with its complex algorithms, is designed to reward content that generates the most interactions. This mechanism, although it can be seen as a way to encourage creativity, often results in constant competition for the attention of others. Users find themselves having to produce increasingly sensational or emotional content to stand out in an information-saturated environment, sometimes prompting them to distort their identity to fit what is deemed "viral."

Social media serve as a stage where individuals present

curated versions of their lives. This process of identity construction is intrinsically linked to what Erving Goffman called "social interaction theory": people play roles and construct their identities based on the social context in which they find themselves. However, the digital context amplifies this dynamic.

If users, in order to gain visibility, feel compelled to distort their identity by emphasizing aspects of their lives that meet prevailing social and cultural standards, this behavior can lead to a dissociation between online and real identities, generating inner conflicts and confusion about who they really are.

The pressure to conform to the aesthetic standards and values of success often promoted on social media can significantly influence users' self-perception. The curated images and sweetened narratives that dominate the platforms create unrealistic expectations about what a successful life "should" look like. This phenomenon is particularly pronounced among adolescents and young adults, who are more vulnerable to external influences in shaping their identity.

Body image psychology suggests that comparison with idealized role models can lead to decreased self-esteem and increased dissatisfaction with one's body. Users may feel compelled to present optimized versions of themselves in order to be accepted and appreciated, which can have direct repercussions on their mental health and psychological well-being.

In response to social pressure and the need to conform, some individuals may adopt coping strategies that lead them to further distort their identity. These strategies may include creating content that does not reflect their genuine experiences, but rather responds to what they perceive as "winning." This behavior can result in a "performative identity," in which individuals feel compelled to maintain a façade to meet others' expectations.

In addition, continuous exposure to negative feedback or the absence of approval can lead to experiences of vulnerability by amplifying feelings of loneliness and isolation. This state of vulnerability can further impair mental health and sense of belonging, creating a vicious cycle in which seeking approval on social media results in negative emotional experiences.

Superficiality is a defining characteristic of this culture. Our self-esteem thus becomes a reflection of our popularity on social media, where the number of followers and "likes" becomes an indicator of our validity as a person.

The Like Effect and Approval Seeking

One of the most significant aspects of social platforms is the "like" effect, which not only serves as a measure of popularity but also as a catalyst for narcissistic behavior. Each "like" received is a form of validation that can generate immediate gratification and a feeling of success. This immediate feedback mechanism is designed to stimulate dopamine in the brain, creating a kind of emotional dependence on these approval signals. Research has shown that people tend to feel happier and more fulfilled when they receive a high number of likes, which further fuels the desire for sharing and exposure.

But many users develop high anxiety related to the need to be constantly approved by others, which leads to increased vulnerability and dissatisfaction.

In this scenario, the representation of one's life on social becomes a matter of strategy, individuals carefully choosing what to share and how to present themselves. This manipulation of reality can affect not only one's own self-perception, but also that of others, creating unrealistic expectations that can lead to feelings of inadequacy and depression in those who fail to meet such standards.

Numerous studies have investigated the link between social media use and narcissism. For example, an investigation conducted by Twenge et al. (2013) showed a correlation between increased time spent on social media and higher scores on personality tests designed to measure narcissism. This research highlights how the use of digital platforms can influence individuals' attitudes and behaviors, contributing to an increase in collective narcissism in society.

In addition, a meta-analysis conducted by Gentile et al. (2012) revealed that adolescents and young adults who regularly use social media show increased anxiety and depression. This correlation suggests that continuous comparison with the curated images and seemingly perfect achievements of others can have a deleterious impact on mental health.

A case in point is Instagram, a notoriously visual platform that has undoubtedly amplified the culture of narcissism. A 2019 study of a sample of teenagers showed that 70 percent of respondents felt pressured to appear in a specific way, and 50 percent said they edited or filtered their images before posting. This behavior not only reflects a desire for approval, but also indicates a growing dissatisfaction with one's image and identity.

The "selfie" culture has led to an explosion of content emphasizing physical appearance and self-aggrandizement. A 2020 survey revealed that 80 percent of Instagram users said they felt inadequate when compared to other users' images. These findings not only prove that social media are not only communication tools, but powerful amplifiers of collective narcissism.

Chapter 4: The perception of reality

Collective narcissism not only affects the way we present ourselves to others, but also alters our perception of reality itself. Indeed, it manifests itself tangibly through the creation of a "curated reality," in which individuals select and present only the most favorable aspects of their lives. This reality is not just a superficial representation, but becomes a narrative to which many conform, shifting the focus from authenticity to performance.

Every post, photo or story becomes an opportunity to showcase achievements, happiness and social approval, fueling a positive feedback loop in which self-celebration results in external validation. However, this practice distorts the perception not only of the individual, but also of the beholder. Users who browse these spaces may begin to believe that the lives of others are always ideal and free of difficulties and experience a sense of inferiority and dissatisfaction with their own experiences.

Psychosocial Effects of Cured Reality.

The construction of this curated reality has significant consequences for individuals' psychological well-being. Studies have shown that constant exposure to idealized images can lead to increased anxiety and eating disorders as people begin to compare themselves to unrealistic standards. Moreover, this phenomenon creates a social environment in which a person's worth is measured by his or her ability to perform and maintain a positive image, rather than on the quality of his or her interpersonal relationships or the substance of his or her experiences.

Collective narcissism also alters our cognitive filters, that is, the mechanisms through which we perceive and interpret information. In a narcissistic context, individuals tend to focus on items that validate their self-perception and ignore or minimize information that might challenge their status or image. This process of active selection leads to a distortion of reality.

The Effect of Confirmation Bias

A key aspect of this process is confirmation bias, which occurs when people search, interpret, and remember information in a way that confirms their preexisting beliefs. This is an innate attitude in human beings, who want to be gratified by their own beliefs and do not like to change their opinions, but in a context of collective narcissism, this results in an increased predisposition to believe and disseminate content that reflects a narrative favorable to the self, contributing to filter bubbles. These social bubbles limit exposure to different points of view, further reinforcing one's beliefs and contributing to a distorted view of reality.

Consequences of Cognitive Distortion

This cognitive distortion affects not only individual well-being but also social cohesion. As individuals surround themselves with content that reinforces their preconceived ideas, public dialogue and critical debate are compromised. The polarization of opinions becomes more pronounced, creating divisions within society and preventing the possibility of constructive confrontation.

Another important dimension to consider is the impact of misinformation and fake news: social platforms not only facilitate the spread of curated and idealized content, but also false and misleading information. The quest for approval and the intention to stand out can drive users to share sensational content without careful verification of its veracity.

Disinformation and Psychosocial Vulnerability

Misinformation, in this context, becomes a double-edged sword. On the one hand, it fuels narcissistic narratives, allowing individuals to promote distorted versions of reality that can benefit their image. On the other hand, it creates confusion and disorientation among the masses, leading to a growing distrust of the media and institutions. The psychological vulnerability of individuals can be exacerbated by disinformation, as people, feeling helpless in the face of an increasingly complex and chaotic reality, can take refuge in simplistic and reassuring narratives. This leads to a spiral of anxiety and frustration as individuals seek clear answers in a confusing information landscape.

Finally, it is essential to recognize that reality is not just an objective fact, but a social construction influenced by cultural norms, interpersonal relationships and, in particular, collective narcissism. Our perception of reality is deeply interconnected with the social narratives and behavior patterns that emerge in our daily interactions.

Reflections on Authenticity and Meaning

Recognizing that reality is a social construction also involves reflecting on authenticity and the meaning we attach to our experiences. In a context of collective narcissism, it is crucial to question how we can rediscover authenticity in our interactions and how we can foster an environment in which truth, empathy and human connection are central to our experience.

Interlude

Are we all therefore narcissists?

A legitimate question that cannot be answered unequivocally or superficially. The issue is complex, and narcissism is a concept that exists on a wide spectrum, from mild and adaptive traits to more severe and dysfunctional manifestations.

Narcissism can be defined as excessive self-interest, a need for admiration, and a lack of empathy for others. In its mildest form, it can manifest as a healthy sense of self-worth, while in more severe forms, it can escalate into personality disorders, such as Narcissistic Personality Disorder (NPD).

We said that contemporary culture, characterized by the proliferation of social media and the celebration of individualism, has contributed to an increase in narcissistic behavior. Digital environments, in particular, foster attention-seeking and approval, prompting people to present idealized versions of themselves. This context can lead to the belief that narcissistic behaviors are the norm, encouraging the adoption of narcissistic traits even in individuals who, in the absence of such influences, might not manifest them.

But collective narcissism is a concept that differs from individual narcissism. While the former relates to the orientation of a society, the latter refers to self-interest and the need for individual approval. Certainly we live in a society in which collective narcissism has influenced the behavior of many individuals. However, this does not imply that every person is a narcissist in the clinical sense of the term.

Many of us may exhibit narcissistic traits without having a narcissistic personality disorder. These traits may include a desire for recognition, attention to one's appearance and a search for social approval. But when these behaviors result in a lack of empathy, exploitation of others, or a constant need for adoration, here we approach more severe manifestations of narcissism.

Awareness is a key key to understanding and coping with narcissism. Recognizing one's narcissistic behaviors and attitudes is a first step toward greater authenticity and genuine connection with others.

Ultimately, the answer to the question of whether we are all narcissists is not a simple "yes" or "no." It is important to recognize that, in a culture that promotes and amplifies narcissism, many of us may develop narcissistic traits to varying degrees. However, this does not mean that everyone is a narcissist in the pathological sense of the term. Awareness, reflection and commitment to creating relationships with others that are deep and genuine are essential to navigating through this complexity.

Collective Narcissism and Empathic Crisis

Empathy, understood as the ability to put oneself in the shoes of others and understand their emotions, is severely compromised in a culture that privileges the ego. Narcissism leads people to focus on their own needs and desires, reducing their ability to feel and respond to the suffering of others. The result is a less cohesive and more alienated society, in which social bonds are weakened and indifference to others increases.

This empathic crisis manifests itself in several ways. First, there is a growing disconnect to the difficulties affecting others. People, often immersed in their social representation and their quest for validation, have no time or energy to worry about the systemic problems or social injustices that plague society. Global crises-such as poverty, forced migration, and climate change-are perceived as distant phenomena disconnected from their own experience.

Second, empathy is compromised by the tendency to objectify people and situations. Narcissism, in fact, pushes people to see others not as autonomous individuals with emotions and needs, but as tools through which to strengthen their own self-esteem. Interpersonal relationships become merely instrumental, aimed at personal gratification rather than the creation of deep and lasting bonds.

In an ego-dominated society, the capacity for dialogue and cooperation is drastically reduced. The tendency to focus on the self and value only one's own beliefs and opinions leads to increasing polarization. Groups and individuals become increasingly rigid in their positions, rejecting confrontation with anyone who has different ideas.

This phenomenon is evident in the rise of political tribalism, characterized by fanatical adherence to specific ideologies or leaders. Polarized political movements often use narcissistic rhetoric to attract followers, focusing on glorifying the group they belong to and demonizing the other. The culture of narcissism promotes extreme individualism, weakening community ties and fostering social fragmentation.

Chapter 5: Sociocultural reflections and future impacts

The reflections we have explored open the way for several considerations, for example, the impact globalization and cultural hybridization have on the spread of collective narcissism. Globalization has not only accelerated the flow of information, but has also led to the spread of consumption and success patterns that foster self-promotion and self-image. Around the world, different cultures adopt the same narcissistic patterns that emerge through the use of social media and consumerism. Local identities are often overwhelmed by global standards, and collective narcissism becomes a phenomenon that knows no geographic or cultural boundaries.

Above all, we have not considered that social platforms also have a paradoxical effect: that on the one hand they create instant connections and on the other hand they foster deep alienation. Hyperconnectedness, paradoxically, seems to have the effect of isolating individuals in their search for social approval and confirmation, disincentivizing authentic and deep relationships. This leads us to reflect on how collective narcissism may be a defensive response to the loneliness many feel in a hyperconnected world.

However, seeing it as a defense mechanism, not only individual but collective, should not make us more compliant. Nevertheless, it is true that in a social and political context characterized by economic uncertainty, climate change, and instability, the emphasis on the self could be a psychological response to the lack of control and security. Self-aggrandizement and the search for recognition could act as emotional anchors in a reality perceived as unstable or threatening. In this sense, collective narcissism could be seen as a mass reaction to feelings of powerlessness and vulnerability.

An important reflection concerns the future and the impact this kind of narcissism will have on younger generations and those to come. What will be the long-term effects of perpetuating a culture that encourages self-promotion, competition, and superficiality? We may see a generation that will suffer from even higher levels of anxiety, depression and emotional disconnection.

Automation, emerging technologies such as artificial intelligence, and the development of chatbots and virtual assistants that adapt to individual preferences are likely to further reinforce narcissistic tendencies. Recommender systems, which offer content based on personal preferences, may create a narcissistic bubble in which individuals see only what is in tune with their taste or worldview. This could lead to further ego reinforcement as people live in digital realities tailored to them and eliminate confrontation with different views.

Narcissistic consumerism, driven by the need to show off and possess the latest trendy item, has huge implications in terms of environmental resources. The "me" culture not only consumes authentic relationships and values, but also planetary resources. Someday we may find ourselves pondering whether collective narcissism represents one of the hidden causes of the environmental crisis.

The fundamental question that emerges is: Are we as a collective able to recognize and counter the narcissistic tendencies that infiltrate every aspect of our lives, or will we continue to be captured by these self-referential dynamics? This will be one of the main questions we will face in the years to come.

Chapter 6: Impact on mental health

In this chapter, we will explore the relationship between collective narcissism and the increase in conditions such as anxiety and depression, as well as the effects of social pressure on psychological well-being and the integrity of interpersonal relationships.

The intersection of collective narcissism and mental health is an area of growing interest to researchers. Several studies have shown that exposure to narcissistic content, whether through one's own practices or those of others, can contribute to a range of mental disorders.

Increased Anxiety

Anxiety is one of the symptoms most frequently associated with collective narcissism. Individuals who feel they are constantly competing for approval and recognition may develop a form of social anxiety that manifests itself in excessive worries about their own image and the perception of others. Obsession with social approval and fear of not living up to expectations can lead to states of anxiety, which in turn negatively affect daily functioning.

Increased Depression

Similarly, collective narcissism has been linked to increased depressive symptoms. Frustration resulting from not receiving the desired attention or the knowledge that one is not living a life as idealized as those of others, as represented on social media, can lead to feelings of inadequacy and sadness. This phenomenon occurs particularly among young people, who are often exposed to unrealistic standards and may feel overwhelmed by the pressure to maintain a certain image that, being unrealistic often turns out to be unattainable.

The Impact of Performance

The need to "perform" and appear a certain way can be a source of stress and anxiety. People may feel compelled to present a version of themselves that is always positive, fun and accomplished. This effort to maintain a perfect image can lead to a disconnect from one's authenticity and create internal conflict and a feeling of alienation.

Effects on Physical Health

Social pressure not only affects mental health, but can also affect physical health. Chronic stress, resulting from the need to conform to unrealistic standards, can manifest itself in physical symptoms such as fatigue, sleep disturbances, and gastrointestinal problems. This condition creates a vicious cycle, in which physical discomfort further contributes to a decrease in psychological well-being.

Another key aspect to consider is how collective narcissism affects interpersonal relationships. The competitive and superficial nature of interactions fueled by this phenomenon can lead to fragile and unsatisfying relationships.

Decreased Empathy

Collective narcissism tends to reduce individuals' capacity for empathy, as the focus is constantly on self and self-image. This inevitably leads to superficial relationships: interactions become more focused on how each individual can benefit from the relationship, rather than on a genuine interest in the well-being of the other. Competition for attention and approval can lead to interpersonal conflicts. Individuals may perceive others as rivals rather than collaborators or friends, fueling tensions and misunderstandings. This competitive environment can create a spiral of dissatisfaction and conflict, compromising the quality of relationships.

If you find yourself struggling with symptoms of anxiety or depression, it is crucial not to ignore these signs. Your mental health is paramount. Talk to a therapist or psychologist. A mental health professional can offer you support, tools and strategies for dealing with anxiety and depression effectively. In some cases, symptoms of anxiety and depression may require medical intervention. A doctor can assess your situation and, if necessary, advise you on medication treatments or other interventions. Also, sharing your feelings with friends, family or support groups can ease the burden you feel. Integrate activities that promote your mental well-being into your daily life, such as exercise, meditation, or even simple walks in nature. These can have a positive impact on your mood and anxiety. Remember that asking for help is an act of strength, not weakness. Treat yourself with compassion and recognize that healing is a process that takes time. Do not neglect the signals from your body and mind.

Chapter 7: Collective Narcissism and Politics.

Collective narcissism is deeply inherent in the contemporary political landscape. Over time, it has influenced power dynamics, the formation of public opinion, and citizen participation in social movements. Collective narcissism contributes to polarization and tribalism in modern societies.

Collective Narcissism in the Political Context.

Collective narcissism manifests itself in the political context through a quest for approval and recognition that can transcend the individual and be reflected on a social scale. This phenomenon results in a culture in which personal values are often placed above collective ones, creating divisions within society. Political campaigns and public discourse have become increasingly characterized by emotional overtones and appeals to personal identification rather than genuine discussion of issues of public concern.

Polarization and Tribalism

Political polarization is one of the most visible effects of collective narcissism. In a climate in which "me" is made the center of attention, social groups tend to identify themselves more and more rigidly, creating a strong sense of belonging that can result in tribalism. This behavior leads to a black-and-white worldview in which opposing positions are not only contested but demonized.

The Emotional Resonance of Polarization

Emotions play a central role in polarization. People feel more motivated to take the side that reflects their personal ideal, rather than trying to find common ground. Political messages that evoke fear, anger or outrage may be more engaging and shareable than those that promote mutual understanding and dialogue. As a result, citizens may become more susceptible to believing polarizing narratives, feeding the cycle of conflict and division.

The Impact of Social Media

Social media amplify polarization. Platforms such as Facebook and Twitter create "echo chambers," where users are predominantly exposed to opinions similar to their own, reinforcing their beliefs and reducing tolerance for different ideas. This environment fosters the spread of misinformation and the reinforcement of stereotypes, further contributing to social division.

Charismatic and Narcissistic Leaders

In the contemporary political context, narcissism is often embodied by leaders who lead movements and campaigns. Charismatic and narcissistic leaders can deeply influence collective perceptions and shape political narratives. These leaders tend to possess distinctive traits that make them attractive to the public. They are often skilled orators, able to arouse intense emotions and attract attention. They use their personal charm to gain support and build a passionate support base. However, their leadership style is often characterized by a disregard for democratic norms and an obvious lack of empathy.

Examples of Charismatic Leaders

Numerous historical and contemporary examples of charismatic and narcissistic leaders have emerged in the global political landscape. Figures such as Donald Trump, Jair Bolsonaro, and Vladimir Putin have used their strong personalities to mobilize the masses and justify often divisive policies. These leaders have presented themselves as saviors, promising to restore power and dignity to their supporters, often at the expense of social cohesion and democracy itself. The impact of these leaders on politics is profound. Their rhetoric fuels division and confrontation, undermining the values of collaboration and mutual understanding. Under their leadership, political movements tend to focus more on personality and image than on concrete programs and policies.

To counter these effects, it is crucial to foster a culture of collective responsibility.

Chapter 8: Strategies to combat collective narcissism

In a social context permeated by collective narcissism, it becomes crucial not only to recognize and address this tendency, but also to develop active strategies to counter it. Therefore, this chapter will explore innovative and thoughtful approaches to address collective narcissism, with the goal of promoting profound change at both the personal and societal levels.

1. Recognizing Collective Narcissism.

The first step in addressing collective narcissism is awareness. Recognizing how narcissism manifests itself in our daily lives is critical to beginning a journey of change. Here are some practical strategies:

- **Critical observation of behaviors**: In addition to the self-assessment test already proposed, take an inventory of your daily interactions, both online and offline. Ask yourself, "Am I seeking approval or validation from others? How is my behavior influenced by the 'me' culture?" This process of self-reflection can help you identify narcissistic behaviors and question your motives.

- **Analysis of shared content**: Review the content you share on social media. Are you sharing authentic moments of your life or are you trying to present yourself in a certain way to get attention? This can be a key indicator of your relationship with collective narcissism.
- **Critique of cultural** messages: Being able to critically analyze the cultural and advertising messages that surround us is essential. Advertising, for example, relentlessly promotes an idea of success related to image and recognition. Be aware of how these messages can influence your perception of yourself and others.

2. Awareness and Self-Reflection Practices.

These practices not only promote greater self-control, but also help cultivate a richer and more meaningful inner life.

- **Meditation and Mindfulness**: Integrating meditation into your daily routine can help you develop greater awareness of your thoughts and emotions. Mindfulness invites you to observe the present moment without judgment, allowing you to detach from narcissistic thoughts and connect with your authenticity.
- **Self-Reflection** Journal: Regular journal writing can prove to be a powerful tool for self-reflection. Take time to jot down your thoughts, experiences and emotions. This exercise will allow you to examine your behaviors and reactions more objectively, helping you identify any narcissistic tendencies.
- Inner dialogue: Develop a positive inner dialogue. Instead of criticizing yourself for your behaviors, practice self-compassion. Ask yourself, "What can I learn from this experience?" This will help you turn moments of narcissism into opportunities for personal growth.

3. Building Authentic Relationships.

Authentic relationships are one of the most effective weapons against collective narcissism. When we strive to build genuine connections, we reduce the power of narcissism in our lives and in our community.

- **Invest in Quality** Time: Spending quality time with the people around us is critical. It creates spaces of deep connection, away from digital distractions. Meaningful conversations can help us better understand the experiences and feelings of others, moving us away from self-centeredness.
- Practice Active List**ening**: Learn to practice active listening. Instead of focusing on what to say next, pay attention to what the other person is sharing. This not only strengthens the relationship but also promotes a culture of mutual respect and understanding.
- **Fostering Vulnerability**: Embracing vulnerability in relationships is crucial. Sharing one's fears and uncertainties can create deeper and more meaningful bonds. Vulnerability can

counter the narcissistic ideal of invulnerability and perfection, allowing for a space where personal growth is possible.

Overcoming collective narcissism requires active and conscious engagement. Through gratitude, mindfulness, practicing authentic relationships and adopting reflective strategies, a journey of personal and social transformation is possible. It is not just about combating narcissism, but fostering a culture of empathy, authenticity and connection. Only then can we build a society in which human relationships are valued and celebrated, with an emphasis on what unites us rather than what divides us.

Chapter 9: Creating a culture of empathy

The spread of collective narcissism has generated an individualism-oriented society in which self-promotion and attention-seeking are the order of the day. To counter these effects and create profound change, it is crucial to foster a culture of empathy, vulnerability and authenticity. But how to do it?

1. Promoting Vulnerability and Authenticity.

In a world that celebrates appearance and perfection, vulnerability is often seen as a weakness. However, showing vulnerability is one of the most powerful ways to connect with others authentically. Vulnerability is not only the courage to expose one's insecurities, but also to acknowledge one's limitations and accept the humanity in others. Vulnerability is one aspect of inner strength, and showing it can be more enriching than we realize.

1.1 Being Vulnerable in Relationships

Being vulnerable involves sharing one's fears, failures and frailties with those around us, without fear of being judged. When people show vulnerability, deeper and more authentic bonds are created. This kind of openness not only strengthens personal relationships but also helps reduce the barriers of collective narcissism, creating an environment of trust and mutual respect.

1.2 Being Authentic with Yourself

Being authentic means living consistently with one's own values and beliefs, without bowing to social pressures or the expectations of others. In a world that encourages one to constantly groom one's image, authenticity can seem like an act of rebellion. It is only by embracing our own truth and giving up the desire to please everyone that we can live a fuller and more meaningful life. Authenticity requires deep introspection and self-awareness, but the benefits to personal well-being and relationships are immeasurable.

1.3 Vulnerability as a Transformative Force.

Promoting vulnerability does not mean giving in to victimhood or exposing every aspect of oneself indiscriminately, but consciously choosing to be open and true in situations that require connection and understanding. Vulnerability becomes a transformative force when it allows people to truly show themselves for who they are, paving the way for deeper and more meaningful interaction with others.

2. The Importance of Community and Genuine Relationships.

In a society geared toward collective narcissism, superficial relationships proliferate. But the essence of our humanity lies in community and relationships that are essential to our mental, emotional and social health. Cultivating authentic relationships and supportive communities can help counteract the negative effects of narcissism.

2.1 The Value of Genuine Relationships.

Genuine relationships are based on mutual understanding, respect, and empathy. They are relationships in which people feel seen and heard for who they are, rather than what they stand for or the role they play. Building these kinds of bonds requires commitment and dedication, but the results are stronger, longer-lasting relationships that improve the quality of life.

2.2 Supporting the Community

Communities arise from the sharing of common experiences and a willingness to support each other. In a society where individualism is exalted, it is essential to reevaluate the concept of community as a place for collective growth and support. This can be achieved through support groups, meeting spaces open to dialogue and initiatives that promote solidarity and inclusion.

2.3 Reciprocal and Non-Hierarchical Relationships.

In many contemporary social dynamics, relationships tend to be defined by a hierarchy of power and status. Overcoming collective narcissism involves building reciprocal relationships in which equality and mutual respect are central. Creating an environment in which each individual is valued for his or her contribution, without competition, is a key step toward a more empathetic society.

3. Activities and Initiatives to Develop a More Empathetic Environment.

Promoting empathy requires concrete actions. Listed below are some activities and initiatives that can help create a more empathetic environment, both individually and collectively.

3.1 Empathy Education

One of the most effective initiatives to develop a culture of empathy is education. Introducing emotional education programs in schools and workplaces can help raise awareness of the importance of empathy in everyday interactions. These programs can include exercises in active listening, conflict management and emotional awareness, all aimed at encouraging greater mutual understanding and respect.

3.2 Empathic Dialogues

Promoting empathetic dialogues within the community is another very powerful strategy. Creating safe spaces where people can express themselves without judgment and listen carefully to the experiences of others helps build bridges between individuals and groups with different views. Organizing discussion groups, sharing circles or events that foster open dialogue can lead to a deeper understanding of different life experiences and help reduce social divisions.

3.3 Volunteer Initiatives and Solidarity Actions.

Participating in volunteer or outreach activities is a concrete way to put empathy into practice. Through volunteering, people can experience the power of human connection and develop greater sensitivity to the needs of others. Volunteering not only strengthens a sense of community, but also helps counteract the self-centeredness and isolation promoted by collective narcissism.

3.4 Gratitude Practices

Encouraging the practice of gratitude is an effective way to cultivate empathy. Being grateful for what we have and for the people around us helps us develop a more positive and less self-focused perspective. Expressing gratitude not only strengthens personal bonds, but also promotes a sense of belonging and interdependence within the community.

There is no question that creating an empathetic culture requires an active and ongoing commitment on the part of individuals and communities. Empathy is the foundation on which we can create a more united society in which people feel heard, understood and valued for who they are, not what they represent.

Final reflections

The phenomenon of collective narcissism is a psychological and cultural force that goes far beyond the superficial behaviors of an image-obsessed society. It is a deep-rooted tendency that alters the way we perceive ourselves and interact with others. It is not just a matter of personal prominence or attention-seeking: it is a distortion of our collective identity rooted in global social, economic and political changes.

This trend is not accidental, nor can it be ignored as a mere phase of modernity. Rather, it reflects a structural transformation of our society, a society that rewards self-promotion, competition and artificial image-making, rather than authenticity and human connection. Collective narcissism, then, is not just a consequence of the digital age, but a manifestation of a culture that invites us to see ourselves through the distorting mirror of others' approval, rather than through the prism of inner awareness.

In the face of these dynamics, the first step for change is awareness. As we have seen, understanding collective narcissism is essential to addressing it. Recognizing that we are all, in one way or another, participants in this culture is essential to begin to defuse its effects. This is not a matter of blaming or pointing fingers at those who use social media or seek recognition, but of thinking critically about how these practices affect our sense of self and our relationship with the world.

But awareness alone is not enough. It requires a real commitment to change the way we relate to others and to the world. This means making a deliberate effort to build authentic relationships, based on real connection rather than an exchange of superficial approvals. It also means challenging society's expectations, which push us to be constantly on display, and seeking instead a healthier balance between our inner lives and our public presence.

Above all, in a society that pushes us to hide our vulnerabilities and promote only a "perfect" version of ourselves, authenticity becomes a revolutionary practice. Learning to be vulnerable, to express one's limitations and imperfections, is not only an act of personal courage, but a contribution to the transformation of a culture that isolates us. Vulnerability connects us to others on a deeper level, beyond appearances, allowing us to build bonds that are not based on judgment or performance, but on mutual understanding and acceptance.

In this context, the relationship with social media needs to be renegotiated. If used with awareness, they can become tools for connection and personal growth, rather than means to perpetuate narcissism. It is essential to ask ourselves, whenever we expose ourselves to the judgment of others, what is the underlying motivation: are we seeking superficial recognition or are we trying to share a meaningful part of ourselves?

We are immersed in a culture that constantly bombards us with messages that invite us to compete, compare ourselves and seek the approval of others.

Remaining vigilant to the narcissistic dynamics around us is crucial. It means paying attention to how they affect our psychological well-being and relationships, but also making conscious decisions about how we want to participate in contemporary culture. The more we question our choices and motivations, the more we become able to resist the narcissistic homologation that pervades every aspect of our lives.

Change, however, cannot be only individual. If we really want to "transform the world," we must also act at the societal level. This means fostering a culture of empathy, collaboration and interdependence, in which the value of each individual is measured not only by personal achievements, but also by his or her ability to contribute to social welfare.

Ultimately, the invitation is to remain engaged in a process of growth and transformation, both individually and collectively.

We cannot escape the "me" culture altogether, but we can choose how to respond to it. We can choose to cultivate mindfulness, build meaningful relationships, and commit ourselves to a more empathetic and inclusive society. Only then can we hope to escape the spiral of collective narcissism and build a future in which the value of each of us is recognized for who we are, rather than how we appear.

Appendix

Supporting Organizations:

1. **American Psychological Association (APA)**: APA offers resources to better understand narcissism and find psychological support. Website:www.apa.org
2. **National Institute of Mental Health (NIMH):** The NIMH provides information on psychological conditions, including disorders related to narcissism and anxiety. Web site:www.nimh.nih.gov
3. **Mental Health America (MHA):** is an organization dedicated to promoting mental health by providing resources and support to address issues related to narcissism and emotional well-being. Web site:www.mhanational.org

Kathleen Lee Dong

Born in 1969, she is a counselor, coach and therapist.

After moving to Boston to pursue studies in Psychology and Mental Science, she delved into the emotional and behavioral complexities that characterize human beings. Her academic training has fueled a deep passion for research and practical application.

Since the late 1990s she has been a contributor for Self magazine, where she wrote and collected testimonies in emotional distress and dealt with issues of relational healing. She has worked as a consultant in divorce law firms and as a coach and counselor for recovery centers. Today she makes her knowledge available through popular notebooks that analyze the link between narcissism and trauma, illustrating and raising awareness of how these factors can contribute to self-sabotaging behaviors.

Take one more step in your growth journey

If you found this book useful and would like to explore other topics related to relationships and personal growth, I invite you to reflect on some key questions:

1. What is your main goal?

- Want to better understand **pathological narcissism** and how it affects relationships?

- Looking for support in dealing with **narcissistic mothers or fathers** and their dynamics?

- Do you want to develop strategies for dealing with **gaslighting** situations?

2. What difficulties are you facing?

- Do you feel blocked by **domestic violence** or toxic relationships?

- Have you experienced **silent treatment** and wish to understand how to handle it?

- Not sure how to introduce **micro-habits** into your daily routine?

- Do you feel confused about your **selective empathy** and how it can affect your relationships?

- Think you have **narcissistic traits** and don't know where to start?

- Have you been manipulated and now pour guilt onto your body with **binge eating**?
- Is your boss boss **bossing** you?

3. What would you like to learn the most?

- Techniques such as ***gray rock*** and the ***broken record method*** for dealing with manipulative behaviors.
- How to create a safe space for yourself through **mental isolation**.
- Different strategies to rebuild your self-esteem and establish healthy boundaries.

Discover Books That Can Help You

Kathleen Lee Dong have written other books that can offer you support and resources for dealing with these challenges. They are practical manuals for recognizing and dealing with the dynamics of manipulation. They are all available on Amazon translated into multiple languages.

For more insights and practical strategies, visit Amazon profile and discover other available titles. Each book is designed to offer you concrete and effective support and is a small guide in your growth journey.

KATHLEEN LEE DONG

IS IT GASLIGHTING?

LEARN THE RULES OF THE GAME

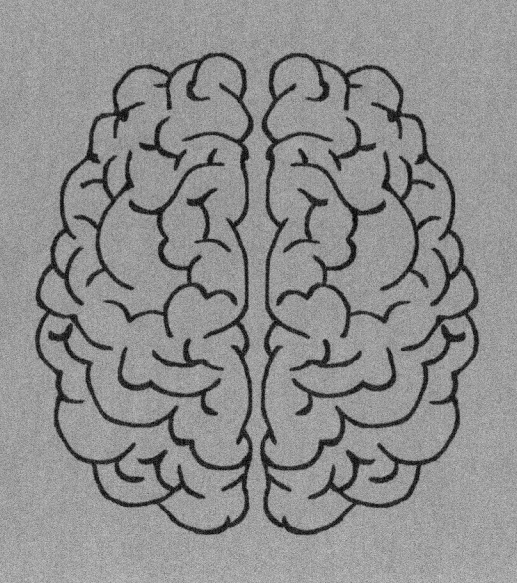

THAT DARK LOOK

EYES AND TRANSFORMATION IN ABUSE

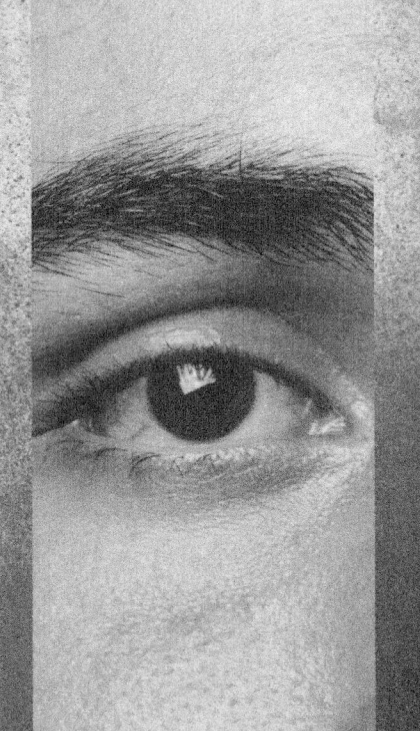

CLIMBING NARCISSUS

NARCISISMO NEL LAVORO E NELLA CARRIERA: GESTIRE IL BOSS O IL COLLEGA NARCISISTA

Kathleen Lee Dong

KATHLEEN LEE DONG

GRAY ROCK

THE SECRET METHOD TO CHANGE YOUR INTERACTIONS WITH NARCISSISTS AND MAKE THEM HARMLESS

KATHLEEN LEE DONG

How to respond to a narcissist
in all situations

Mindscribe Press

Kathleen Lee Dong

SELECTIVE

EMPATHY

MINDSCRIBE
PRESS

Kathleen Lee Dong

SURVIVING

SILENCE

**How to cope with
and overcome
silent treatment**

MINDSCRIBE
PRESS

THE INVISIBLE TRAUMA

growing up with a narcissistic
father or mother

KATHLEEN LEE DONG

KATHLEEN LEE DONG

you killed me

Why do men continue to kill women?

Kathleen Lee Dong

MICRO-CHANGES
MEGA-RESULTS

"THIS BOOK WILL CHANGE
YOUR LIFE!"

How small habits can
revolutionize your life

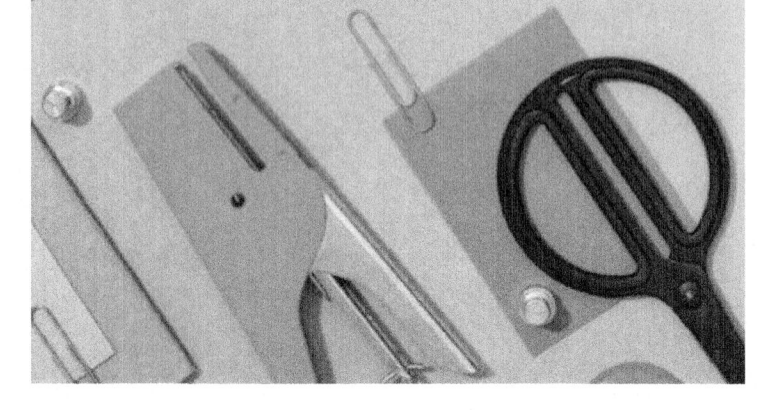

KATHLEEN LEE DONG

Beyond
GRAY ROCK

ADVANCED TOOLS TO DISTANCE ONESELF FROM TOXIC PEOPLE AND PREVENT THEIR RETURN

Printed in Great Britain
by Amazon